OK BOOMER
AND OTHER RADIO POEMS

GRAEME JOHNSTONE

OK Boomer and other radio poems
Copyright © 2020 by Graeme Johnstone
978-0-6488619-0-4

Published by G. & E. Johnstone. All rights reserved. No part of this publication may be reproduced in any manner whatsoever, or stored in a retrieval system or transmitted in any form or by any means, electronic, mechanical, photocopying, recording or otherwise, without the prior written permission of the author, except in the case of brief quotations embodied in critical articles or reviews. Please do not participate in or encourage the piracy of copyrighted materials in violation of authors' rights. Purchase only authorized editions.

The publisher and author assume no responsibility or liability whatsoever on the behalf of any purchaser or reader of this material. Any perceived slight of specific people or organizations is unintentional. While all attempts have been made to verify information provided in this publication, neither the author nor the publisher assumes any responsibility for errors, omissions or contrary interpretation of the subject matter herein.

OK Boomer and other radio poems is also available as an e-book for Kindle, Kobo, Apple and other devices.

CONTENTS

FOREWORD 1
THANK YOU 5
THE POEMS 6
    OK Boomer 7
    The helicopter parent 9
    Perce, the punk possum 11
    Lingering death on the 600 15
    Cruising into hellish waters 17
    Pass the NAPLAN, will ya? 19
    Camera 3 on the old dude 21
    Madness at the top of the world 23
    The supernova supremacist 27
    Just one more thing before I pay 31
    The Fourth has never been with me 35
    Tony, Duran, Ronald and Miaow 37
    Fortunately, just once a year 39
    To walk, or not to walk? 43
    A devil of a job supporting the Saints 47
    Lonely life a student's phone 51
    Ode to our new leaf blower 53
    A horrible Giant of a thought 55
    The disturbing feeling of not being connected 57
    Halloween, and no one to be seen 61
    No dreams down the back end 63
    A cricket fan's lament 65
    The septuagenarian influencer 67
    Don't know whether they can handle this weather 69
    Bidding a final farewell to cable 73
    It's always the umpy's fault 77
    The ultimate solution to all life's issues 79
ABOUT THE AUTHOR 81
ABOUT THE RADIO PROGRAM 83
MORE BOOKS BY GRAEME JOHNSTONE 85

OK BOOMER   AND OTHER RADIO POEMS

FOREWORD

RHYMING WORDS AT THE BREAK OF DAWN

At 5.30 every Friday morning, I leap out of bed, and by six o'clock I am seated at my laptop. By eight o'clock, a poem is written. And by nine, I am reading it out, live on radio.

I reckon that even in this day and age of instantaneous social media - oh, OK Boomer, don't get ahead of yourself - getting something of substance from a blank sheet to air in three hours is not a bad effort. Especially as, for the rest of the week, I'm lucky to be out of bed by half past eight.

It is a ritual I have carried out for the last five years, since I began hosting *Friday Magazine*, a news and interviews program on 88.3 Southern FM, based in the Melbourne suburb of Brighton and about a 20 minute drive from home.

It gives me a chance to amuse, entertain and occasionally outrage the listeners via a variety of topics – social issues, education, finance, health, the quirky things that happen around the world, and the humorous, engaging or occasionally bizarre incidents I have experienced.

Of course, the political world also provides plenty of material. So much so, I have created a separate book containing those poems, plus other pieces. It's titled *Chardonnay Socialist*, and is available via the same outlets and formats as this book.

When preparing for the program, the hard part is settling on a topic. During the week I scour the media - mainly the old-fashioned pillars of newspapers, radio, TV, and the internet news services. Not social media, though. You can't make fun of what happens on social media. It is a charmless place and beyond recall.

Why poetic form? As a former journalist, I started with comment pieces in typical essay style, like a newspaper column. After a while, I realised that as I was on the airwaves, the segment needed to be more dynamic.

So I moved onto a more theatrical style, similar to a radio play. The only problem there was it meant I was doing voices for two or sometimes three characters, and that is not an easy thing to pull off.

But the theatre of that approach led me to trying out a topic as a poem one day, and that set the tone. From then on, it was verse all the way.

A poem is a beautiful thing. It stretches the creator's skills. It can jump from tragedy to humour within a couple of lines. It fills the listener with anticipation. And that, of course, means the likelihood of something rhyming.

Rhyming? Yes, I am an old-fashioned poet. I mainly write in couplets, or in three line stanzas, or sometimes in limerick style. I just can't knuckle down and write in the more contemporary styles such as blank verse or concrete poetry. Even if I start out with that intention, the music man in me emerges after a couple of lines and I simply have to rise to the challenge of making it fit.

Sometimes there is a little bit of squeezing, and occasionally I employ several modes within a work, but I generally stick to the classic style.

This book contains a selection from the poems I wrote and broadcast on Southern FM from 2015 until February 2020, when I aired one about the hazards of being a passenger on a cruise liner as the corona virus was spreading. After that, my wife Elsie and I were promptly sent into lockdown with the rest of the world and the radio program went into hiatus.

OK BOOMER AND OTHER RADIO POEMS

I have included an introduction for each poem, plus the broadcast date, to set the time and background so you can comfortably plunge into it.

I hope you get as much pleasure reading them as I did writing and broadcasting them.

- Graeme Johnstone.

A SPECIAL THANK YOU

My thanks to musical genius Pete Sullivan for suggesting I approach 88.3 Southern FM with a program idea; to station guru Petar Tolich for taking it on board and helping it flourish; to Leanne Cutler and Paul Goethel for their thorough professionalism and joyful camaraderie as co-hosts; to Pauline O'Brien for her constant encouragement to develop this book; to the brilliant designer Shelley Glasow for bringing it all together; and to my inspired wife Elsie who regularly suggests topics for poems, always proves invaluable in projects like this, and - after I fall out of bed every Friday morning at 5.30 in order to hit the laptop - displays an innate, unerring ability to go straight back to sleep.

THE POEMS

OK BOOMER

It's been going on for years. Resentment amongst successive generations that us old geezers born after World War 2 have not only had the best of everything, but are determined to hang on to it until we reluctantly go to our graves.
Well, despite the proliferation of 'OK Boomer', the disdainful phrase designed to undermine us, here's the news. We will.
Broadcast November 22, 2019.

Now that the planet has failed
Someone needs to be jailed
So the target has been set by the doomers

Who the heck are they blaming?
Who is copping the shaming?
Us shuffling old Baby Boomers

In outrage without halt
'It's every oldie's fault,'
Shout Millennials, Gen X and Gen Y

They don't hold back
Or cut us any slack
Saying we've eaten nine-tenths of the pie

That we've stolen their money
And killed off their honey
And cut all their jobs to the bone

And lowered their wages
In cleverly devised stages
To the point where they can't buy a home

And the fires are all ours
In the bush and the towers
'Cos we caused all climate change

And we're long-term deniers
And barefaced liars
Both senile and totally deranged

Big hailstones have pelted
Yet, icebergs have melted
As the sun beats down from on high

And we keep eating burgers
From cows that we murder
While we've let all the rivers run dry

We're all about banking
And super and franking
And the holiday shack on the coast

And just a tad clinical
With our somewhat cynical
Views on smashed 'avo' on toast

Then we get 'em so cross
Talking of profit and loss
And that only we gave life a shake

Then start an affray
When we smilingly say
That the bloke on the moon was a fake

So, we cop it all sweet
And keep chewing our meat
And riding the best waves 'til late

All part of the plan
To circle Oz in the van
Pass us the keys, darl, to the V8 …

The Helicopter Parent

Growing up in post-war Australia, we kids were pushed out the back door after breakfast to play with best mates, acquaintances and sworn enemies, to return only for the midday meal - 'dinner' as it was known then - and then go out again. What we did was of little concern to our trusting parents, as long as we returned relatively unscathed by sundown. It's a different approach these days …
Broadcast March 31, 2017.

I'm a helicopter parent
And though I should, I daren't
Take my eyes off my darling boy
And let him go explore

I can't help myself at all
Banging drum or catching ball
I must guide him down the goodness path
And keep him out of strife

I flap my arms and gently hover
Believe me, it's no bother
To ensure nothing bad will happen
To the apple of my eye

Even when he thinks he's all alone
I can monitor him with my phone
And not let him come to grief
With a stranger lurking by

What's he eating? Is that good?
What's he watching? Is that bad?
Does he have his puffer with him?
Is he feeling glad or sad?

Is that game a bit too violent?
He's gone all pale and silent
As he manipulates the console
With his chubby little hands

Oh, I can't move without him near me
I need him close, so he can cheer me
With his cheeky, toothy smile
And his hearty little chuckle

Is the water a bit too deep?
Perhaps he's cold; feel his cheek
Is he thirsty? I have a popper
With his favourite apple juice

Now he's heading down that track
Darling, wait, please come back!
Take your gloves and your earmuffs
And your Batman anorak

Your very best friend is here
So kindly sit up straight
And blow out the candles
On your lovely birthday cake

Oh, what a good job I have done
Pouring my life into my son
I can die and go to heaven
Now he's just turned thirty-seven …

PERCE, THE PUNK POSSUM

Under the guidance of my beloved, our garden is a beautiful, peaceful spot, which has developed its own eco-system over 40-plus years. It has also become the home for a variety of characters, including one very special one.
Broadcast November 17, 2017.

Deep in our yard, forever on guard
In a nest hidden under the blossom
There lurks near the wattle
Living life at full throttle
Perce, the punk rock possum

Perce is a sight, a ring-tailed fright
For a punk, none said to be cuter
He has a mohawk dyed pink
Silver chains that clink
And a safety pin stuck up his hooter

He's the tattooed king, leader of a ring,
The Nocturnal Garden Marauders
Including a near-sighted owl
A crazed guinea fowl
And a wombat with seventeen daughters

Now, Perce likes fun, he loves to run
Over the roof, leaping higher and higher
But given a best wish
His favourite dish
Is to chomp on an internet wire

It's happened to you, on thinking it through
Remember, you got angry and red?
'Cos a possum did dine
On your incoming line
And made your laptop go dead

What brought Perce undone, the end of his fun
Was the day he came home after dawn
He'd been out all night
Giving the neighbours a fright
And now tried to snooze through the morn

As he took to his nest, poor Perce could not rest
There was a noise he just could not pardon
It was a motoring roar
Revved up at full bore
By a neighbour out doing his garden

Perce leapt from his tree, 'What's this I see?'
Spotting a cord lying luscious and tasty
He grabbed it with haste
Bared his teeth for a taste
The owl sneered, 'I wouldn't be too hasty.'

The wombat went white, the fowl left in fright
A nervy parrot started to stutter
'S-s-top Perce,' he cried
'Y-y-ya gunna get fried
'It's the cord to his electric hedge-cutter.'

Too late came the shout, Perce bit it flat out
And a massive bang rent the air
Sparking flames smoked red
And the smell quickly spread
Of punk possum cooked medium-rare

Perce fell on the spot, his claws raging hot
As with a shower of sparks he was pelted
His mohawk went lank
His chains lost their clank
And the pin up his hooter was melted

The sky was blackened, the house was flattened
The firemen, they duly arrived
Perce's mates gathered 'round
But as one they frowned
Oh, my gosh, he'd somehow survived!

Leaping up with glee, 'What a blast!' said he
'This punk is renowned for endurance.'
But it made him reform
He now rises at dawn
Puts on a suit, and sells insurance …

LINGERING DEATH ON THE 600

'So,' a bloke says to me, 'you want to get from Cheltenham to St Kilda? Take the bus. Avoid the traffic. Sit back and enjoy life's passing parade.' So I clamber aboard the Number 600. And the journey into darkness begins.
Broadcast January 29, 2016.

Motor roars
Door hisses
Gear engaged
We emerge blinking from its Southland cave
An epic journey for the hardy and the brave

In the spirit of Tennyson's men, who rode to their death
We ride the 600
And lose our mind and soul and breath

The bus from hell, snorting and braking
Hands clutching, tired limbs aching
As we roll down the highway
Onto Charman and Tramway
Past home and apartment, office and takeaway

But by Black Rock we have distinctly slowed
And fallen to snail's pace into Bluff Road
Now we have stopped, what's the score?
We rest here for minutes, and many minutes more

Finally, after much toing and froing
It roars into life and slowly gets going
Not even half way
To our destination
Wait, up ahead is that Sandringham Station?
Settle down, son, you're hallucinating

When we reach it, we wait for a mob from the train
And then head off in circles, again and again

Now the beach is in view
Ah, that is better
Get out paper and pen
Must write a letter
To my local MP
To suggest it be better
To run an express
Straight to St Kilda
As well as this route
Made surely to bewilder

'It could be worse,' says a man in the queue
'You should try the number 992
'It disappears down Hampton Street, and Wilson and Bay
'If you make it that far, you get a company bouquet
'Some get down on their knees and pray
'But one poor man begged for the tourniquet'

People get on
People get off
Did that last man smirk as we slowly drove off?
Does he know something that I do not know?
That the remainder is travelled in the gear marked 'low'?

Wait! Our destination is at last looming
Stop the moaning and keening and glooming

Here we are, dissemble that glower
The sun has replaced that last little shower
And the scenery is great
Love that Fitzroy Street flower
But must the 600 take nearly an hour ..?

Cruising into Hellish Waters

As it unfolded, the COVID-19 crisis turned into a humanitarian nightmare. But in the early days, there were elements that had a humorous slant - particularly the notion of being stuck on board a cruise liner.
Broadcast February 7, 2020.

Hello, we're way down here!
Can you hear us tapping?
Our cruise has come to a grinding halt
A sort of virus-spawned kidnapping

We're in cabin Three Four Zero One
True steerage cellar dwellers
Twenty metres below the plimsoll
And four away from the propellers

Yeah, we bought the cheapest digs
But it'd be days on deck, we thought
Then the whole thing turned to crap
Now we're entombed, stuck in port

We understand the seriousness
Sadly, the death count's gathering
But where we are it's so enclosed
We're hallucinating and blathering

My ears are shot, my nose is blocked
And my wife's not feeling great
Last night when she sat on the loo
She started to levitate

Don't know port from starboard
My left hand from my right
Is the cabin haze from the bushfires?
Or am I finally losing my sight?

What's that you say? Start a revolt?
Mount a massive escape?
Can't do that, they're very keen
To keep the place shipshape

Monitors roam the corridors
Like the days of school
You open the door and there he stands
A steward dressed as a ghoul

He's the Baron of the Brig
The Sultan of the Cells
Oblivious to our cries for help
The yearning, the foraging, the smells

Oh, they feed us and water us
Like we're still out on the cruise
But how much longer can you stand
Watching only the BBC News?

My apologies for my whinging
Or sounding so grim and sour
I guess I'd better own up now
It's only been forty-eight hours

But, we're in a cabin of four
Booked with love in our soul
With our thirty-two-year-old daughter
And her boyfriend, just out on parole …

PASS THE NAPLAN, WILL YA?

When NAPLAN was launched, it appeared to be a very useful idea. A regular assessment of student levels in all schools, helping to develop policy, resource allocation and curriculum planning. But somewhere along the line, things got blurred.
Broadcast June 1, 2018.

I'm being set for NAPLAN
The education zap-plan
So my school can prove its worth, and shine the shingle on its door

My teacher sees NAPLAN
As a fine testing snap-plan
So she takes me for extra study, each morning at half-past four

But her face grows kinda weary
As I battle with Einstein's Theory
And as for the views of Stephen Hawking, I'm all at sea

She gets all sad and teary
When I can't spell 'harakiri'
And struggle with the concept of Shinto Philosophy

Her spirits take a dive
Searching my hard drive
For the thesis I had to write on tariffs and trade

And I'm shaking with fear
As she brings out Shakespeare
I say, 'Please, Mrs Brown, I'm only in Third Grade.'

I wouldn't mind it much
This extra testing crutch
If people weren't so serious and full of hypocrisy

I feel bad for my parents
Jennifer and Terence
They think it's for the best, despite my obvious anxiety

So, bugger you, NAPLAN
I think you're a crap plan
A nasty battle of wills to prove which school is best

They've got it all wrong
Time to ring the gong
Shouldn't they be testing to teach, and not teaching to test?

Alas, the moment's here
And I am filled with fear
As I have to tackle every question on my own

Oh, how I wish I was like
My dopey cousin Ike
They know him well, and made him stay at home …

CAMERA 3 ON THE OLD DUDE

A morning TV show sacked its long-term host and then months later brought him back on a million dollars a year. Even though it was half his previous salary, I figured for that kind of dough I'd be happy to sign on and add a certain style of reporting.
Broadcast November 15, 2019.

I know I'm getting older
I know I'm getting grey
But I know what I want in life
To work on Channel Nine's *Today*

I can see they're getting desperate
Locked in a nasty ratings snarl
Things have gotten so bad now
They're bringing back 'The Karl'

Oh, they can still talk of The Now
About diets and attending gym
And whether 10,000 steps a day
Will keep you lithe and trim

But we're an aging population
So I'd add some specific roles
Like super and dementia
And the latest news on Bowls

Or discuss franking credits
And fixing your cataracts
Or the people you need to go and see
About your poor old aching back

Yes, there are lots of nasty things
Hitting us oldies with stealth
Like the pain in our wonky knees
And slipping cognitive health

The mystery of bladder control
Now, there's a topic of the day
And how you reduced the tech to tears
The last time you had an x-ray

And don't forget your hearing
I said, 'Don't forget your hearing!!!'
And that you still want to drive
Despite the motoring public
Taking evasive action to survive

So I reckon *Today* is for me
Reporting with charm and ease
My first report will be on
Obstructive pulmonary disease …

Madness at the Top of the World

On May 29, 1953, Edmund Hillary and Tenzing Norgay conquered Mt Everest, achieving god-like status. Only four more people made it to the top during the rest of 1950s and only 18 throughout all of the 1960s. Now, every Tom, Dickhead and Barry is having a lash. Broadcast May 30, 2019.

It's been a helluva time
But I'm doing just fine
I'm tackling the world's toughest test

To fill a life's aim
For glory and fame
I'm on the slopes of Mount Everest

I'm feeling all right
The summit's in sight
But for now, there's little to do

Got to be patient
Can't get complacent
I'm Number Eighty Six in the queue

It's a huge mob up here
From far and near
All yearning to ascend to the peak

But I'm prone to tears
I've trained seven years
While the bloke in front's done a week

A team of supporters
And four local porters
Dragged him up in a sled from base camp

And the story goes
He won't get froze
To get down, he's built his own ramp

And the bloke behind me
He doesn't mind me
He doesn't need help or guiding

The hillside rumour
He has a sense of humour
And got to this point paragliding

The hero of the show
Is a shaman all aglow
With a performance most highly rated

He preached all the way
Chanted and prayed
And to cross the crevasses, levitated

What's that boys?
Oh, it's the noise
Of a motorbike coming up from afar

It's the 'Sunrise' show
Thrashing through the snow
With its host Kochi in the side-car

TV is everywhere
Makes you despair
Us real climbers are feeling so bitter

Go away, you!
Another film crew
With Joanna Lumley borne on a litter

But I must not fear
Two hours' wait from here
Must hold fast, to say that I've done it

Selfies are the go
But things are really slow
'Cos there's a coffee truck perched on the summit

Wait, erase that frown
Here's someone coming down
Gee, now that face strikes a chord

Look at that hair
That smile of a lair
Dermot Brereton on his skateboard

THE SUPERNOVA SUPREMACIST

So why are we here? What is it all about? There are those who believe a great supernatural being exists. Then there are those who don't. They may have entirely opposing views, but they share one thing in common. They both don't know the answer.
That doesn't stop the quantum physicist from occupying centre stage. Broadcast May 25, 2018.

I'm a quantum physicist
The ultimate narcissist
In terms of the universe
I'm the supernova supremacist

Don't confuse me with the geneticist
Or the boring astrophysicist
And heaven help you if you say
I'm a lowly metaphysicist

I'm the nearest thing to God
I hold the sceptre and the rod
When it comes to daily life
I'm a clever little sod

Without me, you'd be lost
You'd be struggling on your own
Without me, you wouldn't have
A camera on your phone

Or a rocket to the moon
Or a transistor radio
Or a laser, or a taser
Or a PC on the go

Of course …

I clash with certain types
Especially the Biblicist
Who continually says, he always will resist
Me claiming that what he believes
Is wrapped in fairy tales
While I reason that our existence
Is based on figures, charts and scales

I love to get up and at 'em
'Cos its about molecules and atoms
Neutrons and photons
Data, data and datum

I say to the Creationist
Please, will you desist
Saying its seven thousand years
Since we got up off the floor

It's all about the Big Bang
A thirteen billion year roar
And don't ask what happened
In the millisecond before

'Cos, it's my perception of Time
The way it bends and loops
It's not so much when Time began
But how it intersects in hoops

It undulates
It waves
It bends back on itself
The concept of a starting point has been put back on the shelf

You don't need to be a genius
To take on board what I say
Just open up and trust me
And then you're on your way

Into a world of equations
Numbers, letters, figures
Calculus and calibrations
And Einsteinian triggers

As the quantum theory lyricist
I am afraid that I must insist
That what I say is the truth
And none can prove me wrong

So, don't be a nihilist
Or a barking mad recidivist
Peer through the telescope
And join the mighty throng

Come with us for the ride
And let's all sing the song
Until a completely different theory
Quietly comes along …

JUST ONE MORE THING BEFORE I PAY

It is truly written that when you head off to the great, green-and-red hardware store shimmering in the distance, you have the best of intentions to buy just one item. But then, when you grab a trolley, all sense goes out the window.
Broadcast October 13, 2017.

The footy is over
The Tigers have won
The days are extending
There's work to be done

The sun is highlighting
Our garden's shortcomings
Hop in the car
We're headin' for Bunnings

Time to get out of
Our winter slumber
Time we did a bit of a number
On the weeds at the front
And the jungle at the back
And, gee, look at that ivy
It hasn't been slack
It's taken over the place
By creeping stealth
And that aging pittosporum
Ain't in the best of health

So we're off to the warehouse
Full of things so green
A wonderland of hardware
And its own canteen

But everyone else has got the same idea
It's taken an hour to park
And I fear
There won't be enough trolleys
But that's okay
We just want two things
On this fine Spring day
Some new secateurs
And a bag of fresh loam
There you go now
Let's head back home

Wait, look at that elm?
That's got a nice branch
And how about these seedlings?
They'll nicely enhance
The kitchen window
Given half a chance

Oh, I remember now
We need four globes
Two fluorescent
And two big strobes
And some Spakfilla
And a tube of superglue
And what about that gap where the roof meets the flue?

And, oh, look at this
Batteries are on special
And that nice lazy hammock
Will keep us in fine fettle

Do you think this chiminea
Would go well in a corner?
Or how about the pizza oven?
I just feel something warmer
Would spark up the yard
And give it some flair
Oh, and you can never have enough
Of these green plastic chairs

OK BOOMER AND OTHER RADIO POEMS

Look at this soil
It's from an ash-covered mountain
And have you ever thought about
A third water fountain?

That blower looks cheap
Hey, it's a vacuum too
I've got an idea
Why don't we get two?

There's some good looking lumber
So as a matter of course
It's time I bought
My own saw horse

A chisel, a hammer
Four litres of stainer
And how about that
Ten-litre storage container?

Okay, that's enough
Time to get cracking
We've got enough here
To get into fracking

Sure, we got keen
And added some things
But it shouldn't make the register
Rack up too many rings

Ooh, there we go
Ka-ching, ka-ching

Okay, we're feeling, just a little tense
At nine hundred and twelve dollars and forty-seven cents

But think of the fun we'll have
With the paint and the putty
And the aqua blue grout
And, look, we've got enough left for a sausage
On the way out

The Fourth has never been with me

In 2018, the calendar aligned beautifully and May 4 landed on a Friday, the day our radio show goes to air. This gave me an opportunity to examine the Star Wars franchise, and make a very disturbing admission, one that astounds anyone under 45.
Broadcast May 4, 2018.

Gee, I hate to admit it
I hide behind closed doors
I'm the only bloke on earth
That's never seen Star Wars

If I venture out in public
It spreads just like a fever
People shouting down the street
'That bloke's a non-believer!'

Oh, I know a bit about it
You can't miss all the show
Like when Leia says, 'I love you.'
And Han says, 'Yeah, I know …'

I've seen the clever posters
The costumes and the trailers
I saw Carrie Fisher interviewed
Until she left us with heart failure

(God rest her soul. She seemed very nice.)

Seen those weird conventions
The fans all hale and hearty
Seen storm troopers lining up
For a nearby kid's theme party

But …

How can you follow a series
That makes the middle films first?
With scenes of barren planets
That make you die of thirst?

And what's this all about?
A pensioner on forced labour
Alec Guinness toddling around
Swishing a blue light sabre

Go on, shake your head
I have other admissions, too
I never quite got Mr Spock
Nor looked at Doctor Who

Oh, what is wrong with me?
Are my neurons stuck with glue?
Should I live on another planet?
Some already think I do …

So, on this special day
If you've never seen Star Wars
The best thing is to stay inside
And avoid all those hard cores

I've got my day mapped out
My head below the trench
Gonna hire a nice video
Starring dear old Judi Dench …

Tony, Duran, Ronald and Miaow

People's names have always intrigued me. Particularly a first name and a surname that rhyme, or examples of alliteration or onomatopoeia, or ones that sound like the person's occupation. This came to mind when the delightfully named Tony Bartone (pronounced 'bar-tony') was elected president of the Australian Medical Association. Broadcast on August 3, 2018.

I love the sound of Tony Bartone
A name too good to be made-up and phony
He's the doctors' boss who knows how to parley
Like the ex-UN chief, Boutros Boutros-Ghali

Then there's the footballer Donald McDonald
As distinct from McDonald, the Ronald
Who lures you in, to sit down and chow
With the speed of table tennis' Miao Miao

Remember the music of Duran Duran?
And the crazed exploits of Sirhan Sirhan?
Here's a name to fill a stadium with cheer
He's going for the mark! It's Aliir Aliir!

In years gone by, there was Lord Haw-Haw
Who broadcast bad news throughout the war
So here's a match-up that'd wreck the data
What if Lord Haw-Haw married Lady Ga-Ga?

How 'bout Edwin Abbott Abbott? Or Snoop Doggy Dogg?
Or Honey Boo-Boo, or Jacob Rees-Mogg?
Or Moon Moon Sen, or the Viet Minh?
Or that smart-arse dog, Rin Tin Tin?

In a Gippsland town, amongst sea-side hills
You'd find a Laurie Laurence, and a Billy Bills
And way back down the political tracks
First Aussie Governor-General, Sir Isaac Isaacs

Fuifui Moimoi played for Parramatta Eels
While the delightful Grace Grace knows how it feels
To survive Queensland politics amid the northern state Borgias
As did civil libertarian, Senator George Georges

Swimmer Alex Alexander, and boxer Hussein Hussein
Explorer Richard Richards, on the Antarctic plain
Activist Burnum Burnum, and the painter Lister Lister
I wonder if you met him, would you call him Mister?

So, let's all give it up for Tony Bartone
A name I reckon you could never cloney
I'm green with envy 'cos I was gonna be in that bag
For while, Jonathan Johnstone was to be my tag

Instead, they called me Graeme …

Fortunately, Just Once a Year

Christmas? You wouldn't miss it for quids! Well, you would, if you recalled how it went the previous year, and the year before that. How you put all that time and effort into it, and ended up feeling desperate for sleep.
Broadcast December 20, 2019.

Seasons Greetings, Mums and Dads
Especially for Christmas Eve
When you put the presents under the tree
And quietly take your leave

With the hope of getting some shut-eye
Before the crack of dawn
When little feet patter down the hall
Heralding the sound of paper torn

I hope you have better luck
Than our very first toddler scene
When in the dark, a tiny voice said
'Mum and Dad! I think he's been!'

'That's exciting,' we both exclaimed
Sitting up like a shot from a gun
Only to see the bedside clock
Saying it had just gone half-past one …

And I hope it went well
For you kinder kids
On your special end-of-year day

When you got to play
Your starring role
In the Christmas Nativity play

Or, as it is now known, a prejudice-free, politically-sound, acutely sectarian, environmentally-neutral reconstruction of a non-binary historical birth event ...

Better than a nephew
Many years ago
Cast as the third palm tree from the left

He was all ready
For the performance of his life
But, sadly, was left bereft

When, in rehearsals
He went over the top
Giving it a realistic Bethlehem touch

And got thrown off stage
By an enraged director
For shaking his fronds too much

And best wishes to you
Grandparents out there
In these New Age child-rearing climes

You were looking
For that golden moment
In retirement, these'd be your times

But alas you're doing it
All over again
Pushing toys 'round the lounge room floor

You thought you were over
Dressing up dolls
But now you're doing it some more

Never mind,
You're learning something new
In this re-born parenting gig

OK BOOMER   AND OTHER RADIO POEMS

Instead of drawings
By Mr Squiggle
You get life lessons from Peppa Pig

To walk or not to walk?

It's a big decision. An invitation to a Christmas party in your neighbourhood, so what to do? Drive the car and remain upright and sober? Or walk there with your clanking bottles and risk running out of steam on the hike back? Or is there another solution?
Broadcast December 8, 2017.

To walk or not to walk?
Now, that's the query
To get to the Christmas cocktail party
Where the talk will be oh, so cheery

And we'll drink a few bubblies
And maybe the odd little beer-y
But not so many that we come home
Tired and somewhat bleary

But how will we get there?
Which mode will we use?
How will we arrive
With our caché of booze?

It's within striking distance
So Google Maps claims
Nine hundred metres
Is all that remains

Between us and a good time
To be had by all
To talk about the year
Or the bits we can recall

Seven minutes on the bus
Every twenty on the dot
But we're at a bad time
When it's crowded and hot

At our age, must be careful
Not to tarry or lag
Or jump on all flustered
And trip on a school bag

Twelve minutes to walk
Doesn't sound hard
But the old hip is flaring
And both knees are jarred

And last time we tried it
We ran out of breath
My beloved say it was like
Pregnancy, or death

So what about a taxi?
Let's throw that in the mix
Oh, do you really want to suffer
All that Greek politics ..?

I'd like to try that Uber
But you gotta get an App
We need one of the grandkids
To install it and to tap

Look, this is serious
We can't keep 'em waiting
We must make a decision
Opportunity is abating

It's two minutes in the car
Toss you for who'll drive
So we won't be like the past
Pissed before we'd arrive

Let's phone in sick
Say we've got a bug in the belly
They won't miss us at all
Not on your nelly

We'll spend the night in, darl
There's stuff there from the deli
I'll get the drinks
You warm up the telly …

A Devil of a Job Supporting the Saints

After years of torment, misery, near-misses, arguments, heroics, moral victories and furious in-fighting, in 2017 AFL club St Kilda teased all us long-suffering supporters by almost - but not quite - making the finals.
Again.
Broadcast July 28, 2017.

Supporting St Kilda
Is a gut-wrenching role
It hardens the heart
And tortures the soul

As finals hopes go
Down the black hole
We all cry as one
'Please score a goal!'

But those vital six points
Prove all too elusive
Our opponent's defence
Is far too intrusive

They charge downfield
And add to their score
And we shake our heads
Can we take anymore?

All we can muster
Is the famous Saints call
'Ah, come on umpy,
'That's gotta be ball-l-l-llllllll!'

'Get in their boys!
'Man up, be strong
'Don't handball backwards
'Kick the thing l-o-n-nnnnnng!'

Oh, the Saints, they tease you
They intrigue you
But never quite please you
Win games they should lose
And lose ones they should win
Beat the flag favourites one week
Then let a mug do 'em in
So we stare into our glasses
Of beer laced with gin
And swear we won't go back
And watch 'em again

But they lure us back year after year
With hope and belief
Sparking a horrible fear
That if you don't buy a membership
This'll be the year
That they finally crack it and hold up the cup
And you won't be there, for the champagne to sup

From the ghosts of defeat at the Junction
To Moorabbin's sea of mud
To the boutique turf of Docklands
We've given our sweat, our blood

But nothing will be fixed
And we won't get our kicks
Until we relive the glory
Of Nineteen Sixty-Six

Remember Nineteen Seventy-One?
We thought we had that one nicely done
To unfurl the flag
We were all ready
Then along came four goals
From Hawthorn's Bob Keddie

And in Ninety-Seven
It was, 'Line 'em up, barman!'
Until a five goal Crow blitz
From a Darren named Jarman

And worse than the loss of
Two Thousand and Nine
Was that next year we were back
Only to draw on the line

Oh, for five minutes each way
Finish it there and then
Instead of returning next week
And getting done again

So, what is it, that's wrong?
With this club of the Bayside
Why won't it work?
Why can't we go for the big ride?

Is it the players we recruit?
Each board decision?
You set 'em up in Seaford
They treat it with derision

Nowhere to go, they say
Nowhere to part-ay
Too far to go
For a decaf latté

It's time we fixed this
Time to drive it home
Time to get rid of
That loser's syndrome

Too many losses
Too many outs
We must no longer be content
With 'there or thereabouts'

So, come on Saints
Turn this around
Draw a line in the sand
Make us all proud

'Cos, supporting St Kilda
Is a heart-breaking chore
We're tired and restless
Can we take this anymore?

LONELY LIFE OF A STUDENT'S PHONE

At first, I was puzzled when I heard the Victorian Government was going to ban phones in the classroom. I thought that that was already a given. But, no, students would now have to leave their mobiles in their locker.
So I thought, 'I wonder what the poor old phone thinks about that?'
Broadcast June 28, 2019.

Life has changed
Become deranged
Each day now is a stultifying shocker

I'm a mobile phone
Sadly all alone
Stuck in my owner's school locker

It's dark in here
But what I fear
Most as I lie still and languish

Is the awful smell
Straight out of hell
From a four-week old banana sandwich

He couldn't care less
I'm in such a mess
It's like inhabiting a rubbish dump

Two stinking sandshoes
Some illegal booze
And the remains of his asthma pump

Papers and folders
Something that smoulders
And a rather depressed looking carrot

Would you believe it?
How'd he achieve it?
What a place to store his pet parrot!

And what's over there?
Jammed everywhere?
By that unused book marked "Sums"?

I know he adores it
But how did he store it?
His entire Keith Moon kit of drums

Oh, I long for the days
The glorious haze
When he stared all day at my screen

I never left his grip
What a romantic trip
I was his constant communication machine

When the teacher'd say
'Put that away'
He'd say, 'Yes Miss, I will do exactly that'

Whaddya reckon?
Within two seconds
He'd be back logging in to Snapchat

Oh, what have they done?
It's no longer fun
This example of government meanness

But, it's the right call
When you think after all
Most of the day he'd take pix of his penis

ODE TO OUR NEW LEAF BLOWER

We are ensconced in the disposable age. If it ain't broke, throw it away and get a new one ...
This extends to all sorts of household, garden and maintenance equipment. But at home we are still very glad we made one particular purchase.
Broadcast March 2, 2017.

Oh leaf blower, leaf blower, you're our new best friend
The moment we get you started, we never want you to end

So glad that we bought you from the big green store
Cleaning up the garden is such an enjoyable chore

But you're our third version in this long-running tale
As they say in life, some things are built to fail

The first one started out full of promise and hope
Didn't seem to be much with which it couldn't cope

I was so thrilled 'cos it both vacuumed and blowed
A trusty old dog for a leaf-ridden road

But one day it bit off more than it could chew
An errant pile of gravel meant its days were through

Stones got in the duct, and the motor was blown
And on to the hard rubbish, well, it was thrown

The next one we bought was an absolute blaster
Couldn't blow any stronger, longer or faster

Sleek and strong and painted yellow and blue
Looked like a Dalek laser gun out of Doctor Who

No vacuum on this, just brute force times two
Twice it took out the neighbour's shih tzu

But it came to an end when its power cord
Snapped its three-point plug and fell on its sword

And now it lurks moodily in the back of the shed
Miserable, silent, powerless and dead

Waiting for its turn to be thrown away
What a wasteful world we inhabit these days

So we've gone refined, got a version far less brutal
Where the others growled, this is more of a tootle

Doesn't huff and puff like Hurricane Katrina
Does a great job, but is far less meaner

Before I embarrass it with too much flattery
I just want to say, I love its lithium iron battery

And really, does a person need anything larger
Than a perfectly adequate eighteen volt charger?

But the best thing of all, and this is really cool
No longer will I drape a power cord into the pool

And risk shocking myself, and ending up a ghoul
Hearing those chilling last words, "You silly old fool!"

A Horrible Giant of a Thought

On the eve of the 2019 AFL Grand Final, storm clouds were brewing for us hard-nosed Victorian dinosaurs - old geezers who reckoned the game was ruined the day that the goal umpires stopped wearing their laboratory coats. Now, not only were there eight interstate teams, but one of them, Greater Western Sydney - just into its eighth season - was challenging Richmond for the flag. Broadcast September 27, 2019.

What's happened to our game?
Out of Marngrook it came
And a Victorian set up the rules, didn't he?

Now, I'm full of woe
There's a chance the flag might go
To some kids from the back-blocks of Sydney

They've got a captain on one leg
A ruckman shaped like a keg
And many look like they just got out of the nursery

Then there's a Shaw
A Kennedy, a Kelly, a de Boer
And this result will only be precursory

For their full-forward's a gun
They take the ball and run
And they defend like buggery to the bell

They're spirited, fast and keen
Occasionally a trifle mean
And there's a little bloke that goes like a gazelle

So, what is Greater Western Sydney?
It's an area like a mis-shapen kidney
Down the M4, inland from the Harbour City

Two million make its foundations
From a hundred and seventy nations
Speaking everything from Tagalog to Hindi

And as Lucky Starr would say … there's …

Penrith, Liverpool, Mulgoa, Camden
Macquarie Fields, Campbelltown, Liverpool, Granville

Fairfield, Prospect, Bankstown, Cabramatta
Seven Hills, Baulkham Hills, Castle Hill, Parramatta

Riverstone, Cumberland, Blacktown, Holsworthy
Mount Druitt, Canterbury, Bankstown, Hawkesbury

Not forgetting Richmond
But not the one they'll play tomorrow

So why should I worry?
Why get in a flurry?
Why go 'round muttering morbid complaints

Well, it will be their first cup
After just eight years from which they'll sup
And that'll put them on the same level as my Saints

THE DISTURBING FEELING OF NOT BEING CONNECTED

For those of who grew up post-war when there might be one, may be two, families in the street boasting a telephone, the internet is a world we could only fantasize about in sci-fi comics. But now that it is so much part of our lives, things can get very tense when it lets you down. Broadcast October 20, 2017.

Why are the lights on my modem blinking?
Their unstable display gives me that sinking
Feeling in the stomach that I'm off the air
Gazing at the screen with a vacant stare
Bereft of contact with the world
Into internet darkness I've been hurled

Have you ever had to live without the net?
Have you ever felt what's it like to get
That awful message saying, 'You're not connected.'
Your hopes and dreams, they've been misdirected
Give it up pal, you're on your own
Go and amuse yourself and buy a drone.

No, no, no.
This can't be true.
I'm hooked on cyber space, through and through.

Think of the info that I'm missing
Think of the my mail box filling, filling
With stuff that's true and stuff that's furphy
Oh, not forgetting my mate Dan Murphy
Plus the very latest cruising deal
And things that will help me heal
My body and my soul and all that ails
As long as I give 'em my bank details

This can't go on
It's a real car crash
I'm covered all over in a nervous rash

So what to do? Phone Bigpond to get a clue?
No, no. Been there before, pressing buttons
And listening to a robotic voice
Asking you to make choice after choice
Before you get to a person that's free
And then I know what they'll tell me

They've instructed me before
I have to get down there on the floor
And unscrew the cable at the wall
And then stand up straight and tall
And detach the cable from the modem
And turn the whole thing off and wait a moment

Then get back down on the floor
And screw the cable in once more
And hitch it onto the modem again
And turn it all back on, my friend

So I do that, and it makes no difference
The lights are still flashing, which is more than an inference
That it hasn't worked, so I get down and refuse to yield
Lost in my iCloud killing field

Three days later, still no solid lights to see
My eyes are red
I'm deaf in one ear
My arthritis is killing me
As I creakily get down on the floor
And pull it all apart just once more

Enough! Let's ring Bigpond and point the bone
Yeah, waste forty minutes on the phone
Going through numbers to speak to someone
I hate doing this, but it has to be done
Gloomily I take the phone and dial
Expecting a long and tedious trial

But the call is over in forty seconds
'Is this phone connected to your Bigpond account?' the recorded voice beckons
'Yes,' I say, thinking, no need to fret
'Are you ringing about a problem with the net?'
'Yes,' I say, thinking, now we're flying high
'It's a pre-planned outage for essential work, and service will return at 7pm on October 19. Goodbye!'

The voice is gone before I can ask the question
Before I go crazy and berserk
'Why didn't ya tell me that four days ago before you started the bloody work?'

HALLOWEEN, AND NO ONE TO BE SEEN

Halloween in Australia has risen from a non-event thirty years ago to a serious outing. While many condemn it as yet another example of 'Americanisation', in fact it began in Ireland. Either way, we have come to expect the October 31 knock on the door. But this time around, while prepared for Trick or Treat, it proved to be an anti-climax for me. Broadcast November 1, 2019.

I strode back and forth in anticipation
Like Estragon waiting for Godot
I'd filled a bowl with sugary treats
For Halloween, I was set to go

I anxiously went to the window
Peered through the moonlight gleam
But by ten o'clock it was over for me
At my door, no one had been seen

Where were all the neighbouring kids
Strutting 'round in ghostly regalia?
A little tear fell from my eye
I was an October 31 failure

Not one witch, not one wizard
Not a wannabe Michael Jackson
Nor a blood-stained zombie, nor a wailing ghost
Nor the bunny from 'Fatal Attraction'

Where was the kid with the Pumpkin Head?
Or dressed like a Graveyard Bride?
Or the grimmest of Reapers, or the creepiest Clown?
Or the Headless Horseman on a ride?

Not a Broken Doll, or a Hound from Hell
Or a Voodoo Magic Practitioner
Or a Ghostbuster, or a Beetlejuice
Or from the Addams Family, Morticia

And where was he when I needed him most?
I'm talking about Freddie Krueger
Or his partner in bloodthirsty crime
From Romania, the toothsome Dracula

Was it my fault, this awful no-show?
Perhaps my treats were something to dread
(Anyone want a Sherbert Fizzy ..?)
Or because instead of Halloween
I refer to it as the Day of the Dead?

Perhaps, I too, should've got dressed up
Instead of just being plain old me
Trouble is, even on the best of days
I resemble an Asylum Escapee …

NO DREAMS DOWN THE BACK END

It sounds a great idea, doesn't it? Flying from New York to Sydney non-stop. To prove that it could be done, Qantas chief Alan Joyce stepped aboard with a group of fifty or so executives and guests. But they appeared to be all up the front in splendid luxury. What would the real 19-hour journey be like, down back with the hoi polloi? Broadcast, October 25, 2019.

It's been eighteen hours straight flying
Since we left New York for Sydney
I've lost most of my sight, can't feel my tongue
Have only half the function of my kidneys

Everyone else went straight up front
To revel in Business and First Class
Me, I'm living the actual journey
Stuck down in the Dreamliner's arse

I tell ya, doing this in Economy
Is far from glamorous and sunny
In the last row, smack in the middle
With your back to the wall of the dunny

You try flying ten thousand miles
With your head glued to your knees
And five year old triplets roaming the aisle
One with an off-putting sneeze

And how's the feller next to me?
He's stolen my rug and my pillow
Can't really say much about it
He's three hundred and twenty-two kilos

Another claims he talks to the Creator
Says he's a most accommodating bloke
While the woman next to him loudly complains
'If he exists, he'd allow me to smoke'

I've played thirty-one games of Solitaire
I've watched 'Frozen' fourteen times
Now my tinnitus is playing up badly
Like the Hunchback of Notre Dame's chimes

When they made us do our stretches
I blew an abdominal muscle
I tell you, this world's longest flight
Is a pre-fabricated PR hustle

So, the pilot made a 'chute from a blanket
And jumped out over Tuvalu
I reckon I might try the same escape
And take the drinks trolley with me, too

A Cricket Fan's Lament

Time was, the Indian cricket side was a pushover when they came to play on our shores. Lacking pace and physicality, and relying mainly on guile and spin, they would put up a brave fight before the inevitable defeat. Now, things have changed.
Broadcast January 4, 2019.

Oh for the great days playing India
On our turf we were always winners
Once their quicks had bowled a few balls
They'd surely bring on their spinners

And we'd airily dance down the pitch
And slog them over the pickets
And tickle them 'round the corner
Losing just a handful of wickets

They had such a lovely demeanour
So quiet, smiling and polite
A hangover from the colonial days
Bowing, scraping and contrite

Now, they not only challenge us
They push things to the edge
When they bowl and bat and field
They even bloody well sledge!

They shout, they chip, they niggle
They point and raise a fuss
And what really gets inside our heads
Is they're just as rude as us!

Where once their opening bowlers
Were tiny and oh so benign
I swear to the Don now the shortest
Is bordering on seven foot nine

Their pace makes it tough out there
And few Aussies get off to a start
As we wave our bats at fresh air
And the innings falls sadly apart

Then, to twist the knife further
They show where the game is at
Striding with purpose to the crease
And digging in for hours to bat

Their openers wear us down
Pujara does us so slowly
And when we finally get a couple out
In comes the master, Kohli

He's Sachin and Sunil in one
The star of his own universe
The only way to get him out of a match
Is to carry him off in a hearse

This time a genuine disaster
A historic home series loss
To the men from the sub-continent
Over which we were always the boss

It's a harsh lesson for us all
A mighty kick right up the rear
We thought it'd never happen
But the day of comeuppance is here

The Septuagenarian Influencer

I read that each time social media influencer Kylie Jenner mentions a product on Instagram, $US1.266 million goes into her bank account! As John Lennon said when he first saw Elvis up on the screen at his local cinema, 'That's the job for me …'
Broadcast October 18, 2019.

Gonna be a social media influencer
I think it'll be a terrific buzz
All I gotta do is work out what
A social media influencer does!

It's something about promoting brands
Whether make-up or yoghurt or cars
But they don't seem to be people who've done much
They seem to be people who just 'are'

So I'm working on my signature 'look'
You need it to survive in this rat race
It's either the wide, toothy smile
Or the classic resting bitch face

I'm developing a range of product
Age-appropriate and utilitarian
For a rapidly emerging buying group
The Hipster Septuagenarian

I'm creating my brands with confidence
This is no place for self-effacement
I'm into hearing aids, and walkers, and aspirin
And a bargain double-hip replacement

I was also thinking of braces
That's a product created to enhance
But I don't mean the ones to fix your teeth
I mean the ones for holding up your pants

And the medium you choose is vital
TikTok or Twitter, there's a wealth of them
I thought I'd found the right 'platform'
It was for the 4 o'clock Express to Cheltenham …

Don't know whether they can handle this weather

We organized a tour to the UK to catch up with our son and his family. But as our departure time approached, strange things started happening with the weather over there. How to cope with this?
Broadcast July 26, 2019.

We're heading to England
My beloved and I
And we're looking carefully at the Pommy sky

What's this we see
With our jaundiced eye?
The temperature, for them, is unusually high

This can't be true
It's usually freezing
Full of coughs and colds and violent sneezing

Of runny noses
A sight displeasing
And ageing chests rattling and wheezing

See, if the sun peeps out
They think they're in heaven
As the temperature peaks just short of seven

And the place goes mad
From Durham to Devon
If the tip for the day is a heady eleven

Then in all the parks
There's a sight to be seen
If it manages to hit seventeen

A chartered accountant lying flat
In his Y-fronts and bowler hat
A copy of 'The Observer' as his mat

It's a view that progresses from alarming to horrid
When his flabby white belly starts turning florid
While all around him, children play
With their mothers (sorry, nannies) hissing, 'Keep away!'

And in that land of Pounds and Pennies
It's a miracle if it reaches the mid-twenties

Gotta put a quid in the creaking old meter
To run the fan instead of the heater

But, now, if it's true what we are hearing
Then oodles of flesh must be searing

'Cos yesterday, under the blazing sun
London reached thirty-eight point one

You know what they're like
If they've got that far
They'll try to rival Marble Bar

Some will love it
Some will whinge
Some will go typically unhinged

You'll hear of brave exploits by runners and adventurers
And newspaper pleas to save Chelsea Pensioners

So, is it climate change
That's taking them there?
No, I tell you what it is!
It's Boris's hair

When he runs and jumps
See how it flaps and shakes
A whole new environment it disturbingly creates

You can't avoid it
It's designed to scare
A Brexit-fired blast of political hot air

Instead of gloves and scarves and thermal underwear
We're packing togs and zinc before we land there

Bidding a Final Farewell to Cable

Our house was quick to take cable TV up, when it become available all those years ago. It was fun, it was different, it was interesting, but after two decades it became samey. One day, we asked ourselves, 'What are we really getting out of this? Apart from Escape to the Country?'
Broadcast January 18, 2019.

After twenty years of ebb and swell
Of watching loyally, full-on, pell-mell
Observing stories from heaven
And yarns from hell
We decided to hit the button 'Disable'
And terminate our time with cable

'Please, no,' said their man, 'why the change of heart?
'You've been subscribing with us since right from the start
'Show us some mercy, extend us some pity'
I said, 'How many times can you watch Sex & The City?'

In our case, none

And that was the trouble
Channel after channel of hubble and bubble
Searching for TV gold among the re-run rubble
After a while you start to see double-up double

Truckers and muckers and trickers and pickers
Tattoo disasters and bake-off bickers

City Poms going country in a whirl of division
You know they're never gonna make a decision
'Seven hundred thousand just for that!
'I'd rather go back to me council flat.'

73

We liked Charlie and Andrew and the effervescent Shaynna
Turning an old relic into a family entertainer

Andrew giving the clients just a little fright
Charlie knocking down trees with all of his might
And Shaynna painting the lot in the latest off-white

I also liked Fox because of the sport
But I know this year the Saints'll come up short … again
And my beloved says if they become a top club
I can go and watch their matches - down the pub

Besides, I'm not one for basketball
Or the daily grind of the old baseball
And now the premier league's gone to SBS
Don't see much of West Ham in their usual mess

Sure there was golf and surfing and yachts sailing by
And the gripping cricket amid the sands of Dubai
Where Pakistan and the Windies battle hand to hand
While seventeen people sit in a cavernous stand

We tried the movies, not much luck there
There never seemed enough time to sit in the chair
And watch the entire 'Hobbit'
But, then again, it's pretty dreary, so who cares?

Took the drama pack, but it was much the same
Lots of dead bodies in stinking back lanes
In the tradition of the psychological thriller
Following the well-worn steps of the serial killer

Loads of heated, character-building cooking
And many people said to be good looking
But as thin as a piece of flat cardboard
Striding the cat-walk looking totally bored

And before it went too far 'round the bend
'A Place To Call Home' reached a merciful end

Endless Simpsons and the vociferous Nanny
TV doctors checking every nook and cranny

And does anyone want to see again
Series seventeen of 'Two And a Half Men'?

So, we are committed solely to free-to-air
Just press the button, no charge for their fare

Nothing fancy, just the usual mix
Wait, my beloved has just signed Netflix …

Pass us the choccies, darl. What are we binge watching tonight?

It's Always the Umpy's Fault

When you barrack for a team like St Kilda - which in the 1980s finished last five times out of six years - you lose all rationality and look for a scapegoat. And the best target is the umpire. Thus I perfectly understood the frustrated Carlton supporter who let loose after yet another decision had gone against his team.
Broadcast June 14, 2019.

At the footy, over the years
Amid the cheers and the tears …

I've heard fans get jumpy
Get stuck into the umpy
Calling him names like 'maggot' and 'you dog'

Now we've got a first
A Carlton fan's outburst
Saying the whistle-man was a 'bald-headed flog'

Let's pull this apart
The adjective at the start
Picks at the thinness of his tonsorial thatch

But it's not his fault
His hairline reached a halt
It was forecast in his genes when he was hatched

Now, the second word
Oh, so clearly heard
Resonating right throughout the nation

Apparently 'flog' means
In slang, so it seems
A personal act of, er, um, 'self-gratification …'

Need I say more?
Lay extra at your door?
And elaborate without fear or rancour?

Nahh, I'll stay discrete
And turn down the heat
Let's just add that it rhymes with 'banker'

Now, it might be charmless
But really it's harmless
When you see what's on social media

The AFL wants us quiet
Says any whisper is a riot
And live in the land of deadly academia

With no idea about life
The good and the strife
In the sponsor's box quaffing their red

Changing the rules
Taking fans for fools
Be careful, or soon the game'll be dead

The ultimate solution to all life's issues

In the end, everything - life, death, the whole box and dice - comes down to this. I'm not sure whether it was Socrates, Nietzsche or Simone de Beauvoir, but I recall seeing somewhere a phrase that I feel beautifully captures the ups and downs, highs and lows, and cheers and tears of it all.
Oh, wait a minute, I remember now. It was on a subway wall.
Broadcast December 1, 2017.

When all around you
Are in a bit of a tizz
A snarling grimace
On each truculent fizz

Do not get fazed
Calm them in a whizz
By simply explaining
"It is what it is …"

It's the retort of the now
The ultimate solution
Relaxed, avuncular
Even a tad Confucian

It explains all things
Climate and pollution
The stars in the sky
The diet revolution

Our leaders employ it
To ease the friction
When condemning us all
To a newfound restriction

Sports stars utter it
With droll conviction
When explaining away
Their cocaine addiction

But you must not say it
With a smile or a hug
Or in the frenzied emotion
Of swatting a bug

Stay calm and relaxed
At the pace of a slug
With a cock of the head
And a hint of a shrug

It's the best retort
The problem solver
Whether copping a spray
Or facing a revolver

Without blinking an eye
Take control of the biz
And firmly say, "Mate,
"It is what it is …"

ABOUT THE AUTHOR

Graeme Johnstone had a long and successful career in journalism before moving into the world of prose, poetry and musicals.

He gained an all-round grounding on a local paper in Gippsland, Victoria, before moving to Melbourne and working on business and suburban press and then being appointed Editor of the *Australasian Express* in London. In 1978, he joined Australia's biggest selling newspaper, *The Sun* in Melbourne, and is well known for writing its popular daily column, *A Place In The Sun*, entertaining 1.3 million readers over breakfast every morning.

After a stint as Editor of *Australasian Post*, Graeme and his wife Elsie established "The Wordsmith's Shop," which became a Bayside landmark and opened up a whole new world of writing opportunities.

Graeme's first novel, *The Playmakers*, was based on the theory that William Shakespeare did not write the plays ascribed to him. He then authored *Joan, Child of Labor*, the memoirs of groundbreaking politician Joan Child who became the Labor Party's first woman to be voted into the House of Representatives and the first woman Speaker of the House.

The novel *Lover, Husband, Father, Monster*, co-written with Elsie when they lived in Dublin for a year, chronicles the decline and tragic ending of a once optimistic marriage against the backdrop of the collapse of the Celtic Tiger. The book, written in two voices, proved so popular that Elsie and Graeme followed it up with a chilling sequel, *The Aftermath*.

Customers at The Wordsmiths began commissioning poems and songs for events such as birthdays and weddings. Between that and his long-term interest in the musical as one of the great expressions of entertainment, Graeme began working as a lyricist on projects with musician and composer Pete Sullivan. Their first major musical, *Normie*, based on the 1960s experiences of Australia's King of Pop Normie Rowe, was premiered in Melbourne.

Following the success of *Normie*, Graeme is currently working on a cabaret-style musical with a specific song theme.

ABOUT THE RADIO PROGRAM

Friday Magazine goes to air for two hours every Friday morning from 9 am on 88.3 Southern FM, a long-established and popular radio station servicing Melbourne's Bayside community.

Hosted by Graeme Johnstone, it features an Entertainment wrap-up and review by hair and beauty marketing specialist Leanne Cutler, and Finance by financial advisor Paul Goethel, along with comment, music and interviews featuring local performers, artists, politicians, sports people, authors and residents doing extraordinary things.

Graeme always starts the show after the 9 o'clock news with a poem on the pertinent subject of the week.

Southern FM has been operating successfully for 30 years, initially from a variety of locations in Moorabbin and Mentone, and from studios in the Bayside suburb of Brighton since 2015. Under the guidance of a dedicated band, led by station president Cameron Heyde and program manager Colin Tyrus, it has built a solid and loyal listenership via music, news, health, parenting, books, interviews and a wide range of ethnic programs.

More Books by Graeme Johnstone

Available in both paperback or e-book via Amazon and other outlets.

Chardonnay Socialist

A companion book to *OK Boomer,* it features politically-themed poems, including commentary on the 2019 Australian election, some of the unusual characters that inhabit the Canberra scene, and the distinct lack of leadership displayed over the years in handling challenges such as climate change.

The Playmakers

Did Shakespeare really write Shakespeare? Were there other forces at work? Another hand wielding the quill? *The Playmakers* is the first book written in the form of a novel to question the Bard's authenticity. A colourful tale of creativity, love, political chicanery, murder and a deceit that has remained with us for more than 400 years.

Joan, Child Of Labor

The engaging memoirs of ground-breaking feminist, mother, unionist, campaigner and politician Joan Child, an inspiration for all women, who became the Labor Party's first woman to be voted into the House of Representatives and the first woman Speaker of the House.

With Elsie Johnstone

Lover, Husband, Father, Monster

A trilogy

Co-written by Graeme and Elsie Johnstone and sparked by events they observed when living in Dublin for a year, *Lover, Husband, Father, Monster* chronicles the decline and tragic finale of a once loving and optimistic marriage against the backdrop of the collapse of Ireland's economic miracle, the Celtic Tiger.

Lover, Husband, Father, Monster - Book 1, Her Story
Lover, Husband, Father, Monster - Book 2, His Story
Lover, Husband, Father, Monster - Book 3, The Aftermath

www.ingramcontent.com/pod-product-compliance
Lightning Source LLC
Chambersburg PA
CBHW030303010526
44107CB00053B/1793